ECKANKAR
Ancient Wisdom for Today

Available from ECKANKAR:

Earth to God, Come In Please . . .
The Wind of Change
Soul Travelers of the Far Country
Child in the Wilderness
The Spiritual Exercises of ECK

The Mahanta Transcripts Series

Journey of Soul, Book 1
How to Find God, Book 2
The Secret Teachings, Book 3
The Golden Heart, Book 4
Cloak of Consciousness, Book 5
Unlocking the Puzzle Box, Book 6
The Eternal Dreamer, Book 7
The Dream Master, Book 8
We Come as Eagles, Book 9

Also available from ECKANKAR:

ECKANKAR — The Key to Secret Worlds
The Shariyat-Ki-Sugmad, Books One and Two
The Spiritual Notebook
The Tiger's Fang

This book has been reviewed and published under the supervision of the Living ECK Master, Sri Harold Klemp.

ECKANKAR

Ancient Wisdom for Today

Compiled by
Todd Cramer and
Doug Munson

ECKANKAR
Minneapolis, MN

ECKANKAR—Ancient Wisdom for Today

Printed in U.S.A.

Compiled by Todd Cramer
Doug Munson

Edited by Joan Klemp
Anthony Moore
Mary Carroll Moore

Text photo (page x) by Bree Renz
Third Printing—1994

Publisher's Cataloging-in-Publication
(Prepared by Quality Books Inc.)

Eckankar : ancient wisdom for today / compiled by
Todd Cramer and Doug Munson.
    p. cm.
    Includes bibliographical references and index.
    Preassigned LCCN: 93-72027.
    ISBN 1-57043-095-0

    1. Eckankar. I. Cramer, Todd N. II. Munson, Doug E.
BF605.E3E35 1993   299'.93
                                QBI93-1043

Contents

The spiritual leader of ECKANKAR is Sri Harold Klemp, the Mahanta, the Living ECK Master. His inspiring and practical approach to spirituality helps thousands of people find greater freedom, wisdom, and love. His teachings uplift and help them recognize their own experiences with the Light and Sound of God.

1
What Is ECKANKAR?

The natural way back to God is known as ECKANKAR, the Ancient Science of Soul Travel, which is an exact science embracing the purest of the teachings. It is the original of itself and its simplicity, once grasped, is staggering to the intellect. It is the most ancient of all teachings. . . . It is the original fountain from which all faiths spring.

The Shariyat-Ki-Sugmad,
Book One

This earth is a big old schoolhouse. In fact, so is this entire material level of existence called the physical plane. However, we're here to learn more than just reading, writing, and arithmetic. We're here to find our way back to God.

Our teachers have been many: Moses, Jesus Christ, Muhammad, Confucius, Buddha, Krishna, Zoroaster, Socrates, Copernicus, Martin Luther, Shakespeare, Emerson, Einstein, the list goes on. The courses we've taken range from *Who Am I? 101* to *Meaning of Life 404.* Texts include the Old and New Testaments, the Apocrypha, the Torah, the Cabala, the Koran, the *Tao Te Ching,* the *Book of Changes (I Ching),* the teachings of the Buddha, the *Bhagavad Gita,* the *Book of Mormon,* the daily news, and even nursery rhymes.

The purpose of *ECKANKAR—Ancient Wisdom for Today,* as was the purpose of the old schoolhouse primer, is to teach the basics. Many of you have been in this classroom for quite a while now. You're eager to move on, to expand your horizons. You want to better understand your place in the grand scheme of life, and actually enjoy it! So let's begin.

ECKANKAR Has Ancient Roots

There's a common golden thread running through all religious and spiritual teachings. It's called the ECK. It is also known as the Holy Spirit, the Word of God, and the Audible Life Stream.

Though the teachings of ECKANKAR have ancient roots, they are timeless. They're a living teaching. They speak to us through books and through experience in both the dream and waking states. Humans have been inspired by the Holy Spirit to reach spiritual understanding since the beginning of civilization.

Our basic text is the Shariyat-Ki-Sugmad, which means Way of the Eternal. It is the holy scriptures of ECKANKAR. Each chapter of *ECKANKAR—Ancient Wisdom for Today* opens with a quote from *The Shariyat.*

There Is Always a Living ECK Master

Our teacher and mentor is the Living ECK Master. ECKANKAR is never without a living Master. This ensures the religion remains pure and appropriate for the consciousness of the day. It avoids the theological disputes and political maneuverings so common in large organizations. And it allows the spiritual student to see and hear a teacher who has traveled the path to Self- and God-Realization.

Paul Twitchell Introduced ECKANKAR in 1965

When Paul Twitchell introduced ECKANKAR to the modern world in 1965, he separated spiritual truths from the cultural trappings which had surrounded them. Average people could begin to experience the Light and Sound of God while still living a happy, balanced, and productive life.

Paul Twitchell was born in Kentucky in the early part of this century and served in the U.S. Navy during the Second World War.

A seeker from an early age, he was introduced to a group of spiritual Masters who would change the course of his life. These were the Vairagi ECK Masters. While they trained Paul to become the Living ECK Master, he explored a wide range of spiritual traditions under different teachers. The high teachings of ECK had been scattered to the four corners of the world. Paul gathered these golden teachings of Light and Sound and made them readily available to us.

It was these God experiences he chronicled in his book *The Tiger's Fang*. Paul Twitchell eventually joined the Vairagi Order and was given the task of bringing ECKANKAR to the world. He became the Living ECK Master.

By 1965, Paul was conducting Soul Travel workshops in California and offering discourses on the teachings of ECKANKAR. A community of ECKists began to grow, and in 1970, ECKANKAR was established as a nonprofit religious organization. Paul Twitchell died in 1971, but not before he initiated many into the ECK teachings.

The Mission of the Living ECK Master Is to Help People Find Their Way Back to God

The present Living ECK Master is Sri Harold Klemp. He grew up on a Wisconsin farm, attended divinity school, and completed four years in the U.S. Air Force. While stationed in Japan, he discovered ECKANKAR. Initiated by Paul Twitchell in 1969, Harold earned his way into the God Worlds. He later chronicled these experiences in his books *The Wind of Change, Soul Travelers of the Far Country,* and *Child in the Wilderness*.

Sri Harold Klemp speaks to many thousands of seekers each year at ECK seminars around the world. Some forty videocassettes and fifty audiocassettes of his public talks are available. He has authored more than twenty books, and he continues to write, including many articles and spiritual-study discourses. His inspiring and practical approach to spirituality helps thousands of people find greater freedom, wisdom, and love. His teachings uplift and help them recognize their own experiences with the Light and Sound of God.

The ECK Message Is Not Evangelical

There is no desire to convert people to ECKANKAR. Though many ECKists share their spiritual enthusiasm with others, there is an abiding respect for the belief systems of all people. The ECK message therefore tends to be offered in a quiet and steady way. The teachings are written to speak to the inner being, Soul. They don't play off the emotions or the fears of spiritual seekers.

The best way to find out about ECKANKAR is to read one of the fifty books written on the subject. Many of them mention the Spiritual Exercises of ECK, which you can try in private and at your own pace.

What Are ECKists Like?

ECKists come from all walks of life. Their only common denominator is a love of God and a commitment to spiritual unfoldment. They are of every race and religious background. They are responsible members of their community and are not restricted by any special dietary rules, ascetic practices, or dress codes which would differentiate them from their neighbors.

Most people who have come into ECKANKAR have done so because their questions about life were not being answered by orthodox and traditional teachings.

Experience God for Yourself

A cornerstone of ECKANKAR is the value of personal spiritual experience.

Reading a book or listening to a friend will give you only a limited understanding of the spiritual worlds and your role in them.

To master your life, you must apply self-discipline and have a true desire to experience God for yourself. Your experience with the spiritual Light and Sound of God will enrich your life and help you put daily problems into loving perspective.

Defining ECKANKAR

To aid your understanding of ECKANKAR, a few definitions are in order. We use certain words to define spiritual principles, either because they are more descriptive or because they do not carry the same connotation or stereotype as some more commonly used words.

ECK—The Divine, or Holy, Spirit; the Audible Life Stream; the essence of God which supports and sustains all life; the Life Force.

ECKANKAR—Religion of the Light and Sound of God. Also means Co-worker with God.

Light and Sound of God—The Holy Spirit. The two aspects through which God appears in the lower worlds. The Holy Spirit can appear to us as Light, which is a reflection of the atoms of God moving in space, or as Sound, which is the Audible Life Current that carries Soul back home to God. The Spiritual Exercises of ECK show people how to look and listen within themselves for these qualities of Divine Spirit for upliftment and guidance.

Mahanta—The inner form of the Living ECK Master who guides the spiritual student on the inner planes.

Soul—The true self. The inner, most sacred part of each person. As a spark of God, Soul can see, know, and perceive all things.

Soul Travel—A natural way to expand the consciousness, to experience the higher viewpoint of yourself as Soul through spiritual exercises.

SUGMAD—A sacred name for God, the source of all life. IT is neither masculine nor feminine.

This book will give you a brief overview of the religion of ECKANKAR. Please remember that the teachings are actually quite simple and do not require any formal training or academic rigor. In fact, the basic beliefs of ECKANKAR could easily be summarized as:

- Soul is eternal and is the individual's true identity
- Soul exists because God loves It
- Soul is on a journey of Self- and God-Realization
- Spiritual unfoldment can be accelerated by conscious contact with the ECK, Divine Spirit
- This contact can be made by the use of the Spiritual Exercises of ECK and by the guidance of the Living ECK Master

- The Mahanta, the Living ECK Master is the spiritual leader of ECKANKAR
- Spiritual experience and liberation in this lifetime is available to all

2

Soul Travel

Soul Travel is an individual experience, a realization of survival. It is an inner experience through which comes beauty and love of all life. It cannot be experienced in rituals or ceremonies, nor bottled in creeds.

The Shariyat-Ki-Sugmad,
Book One

A Classic Soul Travel Experience

"A single pinpoint of white light appeared in the depths of the dark universe before me. It was far off in the distance but exploded toward me at a fantastic speed, like a brilliant sun racing from the other side of the universe to swallow me in the hotness of its light. Now I flew toward it, like a tiny dot of light racing to meet a planet of unspeakable radiance."

Sri Harold Klemp recounts this classic Soul Travel experience in his book *Soul Travelers of the Far Country*. It occurred while he was in training to become the Living ECK Master. On this visit to the God Worlds accompanied by the ECK Master Rebazar Tarzs, he would learn how the ECK helps people with burdens of the heart. Sri Harold continues:

"It was like flying into the sun, passing through a curtain of light, and coming out on the other side to a world of gorgeous colors. I hung suspended in space, a splendid light (the glorious Soul body) of seeing, knowing, and being.

"Below me lay the dazzling white sands of a beach, with a multiplicity of blue-and-green ocean waters; the waves washed mildly upon the sand. Small birds ebbed and flowed with the tide, mirroring the give-and-take of life. The bright blue sky was unclouded by haze of any kind. This must be heaven, I thought.

"In the next instant, I was atop a high cliff overlooking the ocean. How can one describe the perception of Soul, since, despite this great height, it was possible to see and hear as if my feet were walking in the warm sands of the beach below?

" 'Look, in the distance!' commanded a deep baritone voice beside me.

"Startled, I looked around. It was Rebazar Tarzs, the Tibetan ECK Master, who no doubt was my benefactor in providing this trip to a most beautiful heaven of God. Gripped in his powerful right hand was a stout walking staff of shoulder height. With his left, he pointed far down along the beach, where two dark figures were walking.

"Suddenly, from our vantage point on the steep cliff, the distance between us and the two specks collapsed. Time and space had both crumbled. My spiritual vision jumped to the two figures in a twinkling and showed a man and a woman slowly walking the beach toward us. To my surprise, the smallish man was my friend and Master, Paul Twitchell—the Mahanta. The other person was a young woman in a flowing white gown that billowed softly around her in the gentle sea breeze. Slender, with brunet hair, she stood somewhat shorter than Paul. Pain and trouble had drawn her face into a tight band, and she plodded beside him as if in a daze.

"The two beach walkers passed well below our observation point on the cliff. A cloak of light surrounded us, and Rebazar made the comment, 'This warm light that bathes us is from the Ocean of Love and Mercy. It is the Holy Spirit and is a reflection of the light from the atoms of God.' Rebazar's ruby red robe was barely to be seen in this mist of golden light, which seemed to enwrap me too, although I could not see myself.

" 'This sphere of golden light is the Soul body,' he said, 'the highest of the forms of man.'

"On the beach below, the heavyhearted woman trudged beside Paul. A shuffling trail in the sand marked their slow passage, meandering footsteps at the edge of lapping wavelets. Paul saw us on the cliff and waved his hand, but an invisible screen shielded us from the woman. They inched along the beach, slowly shrinking in the distance. A long way off stood a lighthouse, their destination.

" 'The sorrows of life have cut sharply into the spirit of that young one,' Rebazar remarked, compassion modulating his musical voice. His speech was not in outer tones, yet it came through the electric atmosphere of this remote world of God as clear as a bell. . . .

"The woman had tried to commit suicide, but the Mahanta stepped in to prevent it. For months thereafter, he took her out of the body at night and brought her to this serene paradise by the sea for spiritual healing.

" 'Her emotional and mental repair will take time,' concluded Rebazar. 'Come, let us go.'

"I took a last look at the ocean and the

beach, and suddenly understood that the sparkling, celestial waters of this ocean were inexperienced Souls who awaited the right conditions for rebirth into the physical world. Then, in an instant, I was home in my room."

The following are ways Soul Travel helps us live a healthier, more spiritually fulfilling life.

Worry Less, Know More Love, Feel Energized, Change Bad Habits

What can Soul Travel do for you? The benefits are both subtle and far-reaching. When you realize through personal experiences that you live beyond the physical body, you are released from the fear of death. You worry less. When you realize through experience that you are a creative part of a loving God, you invite more love into your life. You feel less lonely or alienated. When you realize through experience that your life has a spiritual purpose, you will feel energized.

When filled with the excitement and joy which comes with these spiritual experiences, you are more able to change the habits of the past. Instead of exerting willpower or fighting deprivation, you may find old habits often just drop away.

ECKANKAR teaches that Soul is a happy being. It is not guilty of anything. It is the cause of all Its life circumstances. This shifts the emphasis from blaming others to going within to find root causes. And with this newfound strength it is often easier to serve others and not be so concerned with your own limitations.

You Are Soul

The traditional concept of Soul is that you have one, but It is distant from your everyday life and becomes important only when your physical body ceases to exist. The ECKist believes, however, that each person *is* Soul and that Soul is the essential and permanent center of our being. It can never be lost.

The pressures of the modern world make it easy to forget who we are. Our physical senses and emotions become overwhelmed and we lose Soul's spiritual view. Regaining this view is called Soul Travel. And Soul Travel is accomplished by practicing the Spiritual Exercises of ECK on a daily basis.

Many people experience Soul Travel as an expansion of awareness and knowingness: an inner nudge to call a friend, or seeing beyond your current difficulties to a deeper meaning. Others may have dramatic experiences full of spiritual majesty. In ECKANKAR, you learn to prove spiritual truths yourself through personal experience.

Spiritual Exercises Are Different from Prayer and Astral Projection

You can Soul Travel by learning the Spiritual Exercises of ECK. A spiritual exercise is different from prayer because it encourages us to listen to God. In other words, we let the Creator talk to us, instead of the other way around. A spiritual exercise differs from meditation in that a spiritual exercise is more active. The ECKist actively joins in a higher state of consciousness rather than passively waiting to receive it. And a spiritual exercise differs from traditional religious rituals because no props or physical movements are required.

Soul Travel also differs from the now-popularized astral projection. To travel out of the physical realm using your Astral body limits you to the Astral Plane. Recognizing the awareness of Soul goes further. It allows you to explore any of the God Worlds, from the Astral, Causal, Mental, Etheric, and on to the various planes of Soul. These distinctions will be discussed further in chapter 6, "The God Worlds of ECK."

A Spiritual Exercise to Try

The Spiritual Exercises of ECK help you open your heart to the Light and

Sound of God. ECKANKAR teaches over one hundred different exercises, all designed to give you a greater understanding of yourself and of God.

One of the basic Spiritual Exercises of ECKANKAR is to sing HU (pronounced like the word *hue*), the holy name of God. To practice this technique, find a quiet place to sit or lie down. Relax and think about a spiritual quotation or someone you love. Close your eyes. Sing HU silently or aloud for a few minutes and then listen quietly. You may experience the divine ECK, or Holy Spirit. Or you may gain a new insight into your life. These experiences are not the privilege of a select few. With self-discipline and commitment, you can build your own foundation of spirituality.

ECKANKAR teaches that our destiny is to become a Co-worker with God. This means that we will be a channel for the ECK, Divine Spirit, in our lives, giving joy and spiritual upliftment to those around us. The individual is never lost in ECKANKAR. This differentiates ECKANKAR from Buddhism or Hinduism, which describe their final goal as a dissolution of the individual into God. ECKANKAR's respect for the sanctity of the individual shows itself in how ECKANKAR is taught and honors the rights, privacy, and personal space of others.

3

Dreams

*T*he Atma [Soul], living in the
dream consciousness of the psychic
states, enjoys the subtle things of life, as
thought, emotional joy, intellect, and mind
stuff. All this is essential for the bodies of
the psychic worlds, the Astral, Causal,
and Mental planes. When Soul takes mastery over these states through dreaming,
It becomes the supreme ruler of Its own
universe.

The Shariyat-Ki-Sugmad,
Book One

The following story, taken from
Sri Harold Klemp's book *The Eternal
Dreamer,* is a delightful example of how
dreams can help us in our daily lives.
Dreams can give us symbols to work with,
and they can give an opportunity for

Soul-to-Soul communication.

Once a couple bought a horse they named Sid. Their plan was to train the horse, and when it reached a certain age, they would resell it. Of course, it never occurred to them to wonder what Sid thought of all this.

About a year later, the husband had an unusual dream in which he found himself entering a crowded bar. Seeing one unoccupied table, he went over and sat down. A man came over and introduced himself. "Hi," he said. "I'm Sid, your horse."

The dreamer thought this was the funniest thing he'd ever seen. "My horse in a dream, looking like a man," he said. "This is wild."

The only thing that bothered him about the dream was that this man had a tooth missing, whereas his horse did not.

The dreamer and his horse got to talking. Sid said, "You know I love you and your wife. I'd like to stay with you. I've never had owners like you before who could Soul Travel and meet with me in the dream state so we could talk things over."

"Sid," he asked, "I notice you've been limping on one of your hind legs. Is something wrong?"

"I'm having a problem with that foot," said Sid. "It's just a minor thing, but if you can get a farrier to trim my hoof, I could walk better." And they continued talking.

When the man awoke and told his wife about the dream, they shared a good laugh over it. She thought the part about the missing tooth was really hilarious.

Later that morning as they walked to the stable, they saw a crowd around Sid's stall. The ECKists rushed over, concerned for the welfare of their horse.

The owners saw a little bit of blood on the door of the stall, but Sid seemed to be all right. The husband put a halter on the horse and led him outside. "If you plan to ride him, just don't put a bit in his mouth," one of the grooms advised him. "Your horse somehow got his mouth caught on the door lock, and his tooth broke off."

Husband and wife looked at each other. "The missing tooth in your dream," she said. Without another word, they leaned over to check the horse's hind foot. Just as Sid had said in the dream, his hoof needed trimming.

The Dream Master, the Mahanta, sometimes adjusts the dream state so that one Soul may communicate with another, whatever Its form. Since the man might have totally discounted a dream about a talking horse, the Master changed the image to one the dreamer could accept. This is just one of the ways the Dream Master works.

Soul Never Sleeps

Soul never sleeps. It is a unit of awareness. While the body sleeps, the consciousness of Soul is awake. The memory of this experience is often called a dream.

Dreams are as real and valid as the

waking state. They simply occur on a different plane of existence. The reason so many of our dreams are confusing is that our memory becomes distorted. Upon waking, the dream experience is run through the dream censor, a function of our own mind, and we remember only pieces of the event. Or the dream is camouflaged with symbols because of our discomfort or lack of understanding.

The Mahanta Is the Dream Master

The Mahanta, the inner form of the Living ECK Master, is the Dream Master. One way he guides his spiritual students is through their dreams. He uses the dreams of an individual to help work out karma and to impart spiritual understanding. The goal of an ECKist is to move at will between the outer, or physical, world and the inner spiritual worlds. This can be done via the Spiritual Exercises of ECK and by the conscious use of dreams.

Dreams Help
Spiritual Unfoldment

Dreams play an important role in the spiritual unfoldment of the ECKist. They are a look into the heavenly worlds. In many cases, the dream becomes a teaching tool. The ECKist is always interested in learning, and the dream can be a message about reaching a higher consciousness. In dreams our personalities, with their fears and desires, are exposed for us to look at. We admit things to ourselves in dreams which we would be unable to be honest about in our waking state.

Karma Can Be Resolved
in the Dream State

Karma, or past spiritual debts, can be resolved in the dream state. The purpose of karma is to open our consciousness and teach us a spiritual lesson. If we are able to learn a spiritual lesson by having the experience in a dream, we'd have little need to repeat the experience while awake. The main requirement is that we continue our spiritual growth.

This can save a great deal of wear and tear on our bodies. For instance, the Inner Master could move the experience of an automobile accident from the Physical to the Astral plane, allowing the experience to happen during a dream. It could still be a frightful experience, but much easier to handle there than here.

Dream Symbols Are Individual

Many people claim the images and symbols we have in dreams are common to everyone and can be easily interpreted. You can find books in your local library telling you that water means this or that horses mean that. The dream teachings of ECKANKAR do not follow such a simplistic model.

In ECK, each person is a unique individual. Therefore, the dream symbols used by each person are also unique.

Swimming in a river may well have a different meaning for one person than it would for another. The key for the dreamer, then, is to go within and determine what each of these symbols may mean. This can even become a type of spiritual exercise.

Dream Characters Represent Aspects of the Dreamer

The plot and characters in dreams are not always significant in themselves. A chilling nightmare can hold a very uplifting message for the dreamer. For the most part, though, the characters in a dream represent the dreamer himself. These are keys to understanding who we are and what our purpose is. ECKANKAR explains that we are to look for a positive message when trying to understand the meaning of our dreams. The Dream Master is always working for your benefit.

There Are Many
Levels of Dreaming

There are many levels of dreaming. If the dreamer becomes aware that he is in a dream, he may be able to take control of the experience. The dreamer may call upon the Mahanta and request spiritual instruction. Or the dreamer may choose to visit a Temple of Golden Wisdom on one of the other planes. In these cases, the experience can become more Soul Travel than dreaming.

Dreams Can Prophesy

There are also dreams of prophecy. You can view life from above the normal track of time and get a glimpse of the future. It is best, however, to restrict your use of prophecy to your own personal life. The opportunity for misunderstanding the symbols is great. If you dream of an earthquake and then run to warn your friends of the upcoming cataclysm, it would probably be embarrassing when nothing happens.

Such a dream, more likely, is foretelling a personal shift, perhaps indicating the approach of a sudden change in circumstances or consciousness. The dream may indeed be prophetic, but you could miss the real meaning.

Keep a Dream Journal

Keeping a dream journal can be helpful. This provides a bridge between the inner and outer worlds. Most of our dreams are forgotten very quickly. After reading their own dream journals, many people are amazed at how much they dream.

A dream journal also gives us an opportunity to see any patterns in our dreams. Certain symbols may tend to appear regularly. In recognizing them, we are better able to make sense of these experiences.

And finally, the process of writing the

dream down allows us to synthesize and let go of the experience. As this baggage is released, we gain both understanding and spiritual freedom.

The Purpose of Dreams Is to Bring the Individual Closer to the Light and Sound of God

The ultimate purpose of dreams is to bring the individual closer to the Light and Sound of God. In this way, dreams have the same purpose as life itself. The Mahanta can communicate in a dream with the new student who has not yet been able to open their conscious mind to the Inner Master.

A dream is a step on the path of spiritual unfoldment. It can also be an inspiration to the average person, as in Soul Travel. All things are possible. Life is no longer a mundane, random experience.

4

Karma

The universality of the law of karma is one of the chief factors which binds life together, and not only human life, but animal, plant, and mineral life as well. All these compose one big family, with a complicated and inseparable history and an inseparable karma.

The Shariyat-Ki-Sugmad,
Book One

Sir Isaac Newton was twenty-three years old when he watched an apple fall to the ground in his mother's orchard. The apple never really hit him on the head. It did, however, support his theory of universal gravitation.

At the time, in 1665, Sir Isaac had also just formulated his three laws of motion, one of them being that for every action, there is an equal and opposite reaction.

Newton's explanations are usually applied to the interaction of physical forces and objects. However, the same action/reaction principle applies to the forces of emotion and thought.

The Law of Karma Is Scientific and Logical

The Law of Karma is scientific and logical. It is the spiritual form of the physical Law of Cause and Effect. Every action creates an equal and opposite reaction. The Law of Karma helps us understand the effect of our actions. The process helps Soul mature. The law's purpose is to teach love and to uplift, not to punish.

Karma applies itself in the most exacting and clever of ways. If we deprived another human being of freedom in a previous life, we'd probably have our freedom curtailed in this life. This experience would give us time to reconsider our views and learn the Law of Love.

Karma Can Liberate Us from Being a Victim

Once we accept the Law of Karma in our lives, we are liberated from being the victim. We begin to see underlying spiritual causes and act accordingly. Problems become opportunities for spiritual growth.

Karma differs from fate or destiny because it encourages us to take an active role in life. The Law of Karma requires the spiritual seeker to follow the highest code of ethics. The rules are simple. ECKANKAR is not a passive path to God.

You Can Be Free of Karma

When you achieve the exalted state of Self-Realization, you'll still be held accountable for your actions in your daily life. However, you will have worked off the karma built up from past lives. And when you finish your mission in this life, unless you choose to come back to this plane to teach or to serve, you need not return.

Perhaps you will maintain this expanded consciousness throughout your lifetime. Perhaps you'll hold on to it for only a moment at a time. You will learn, however, that there is always a risk of losing the 360-degree viewpoint. You earn each step toward God Consciousness moment to moment.

Most ECKists want to be free of karma. They would like to balance their karmic account by the end of their present lifetime. The Mahanta helps them do this. By practicing the Spiritual Exercises of ECK, they drop the attitudes and habits binding them to the past. They can fulfill their spiritual destiny without having to be reborn. Thus they are freed from endless rounds on the wheel of eighty-four. The ECKist calls this spiritual liberation.

Karma Metes Out Perfect Justice

The Law of Karma metes out perfect justice. This is reassuring in a world which can appear to be unjust. One duty of the ECKist is to show compassion and kindness to all, regardless of their position on the spiritual ladder. We are all on a spiritual journey together.

Our suffering is not always punishment for past actions. There are many subtle processes at work. If you experienced fear and persecution in a past life, you may still carry these feelings in your psychic memory. You may experience unwarranted fear and anxiety in your current life. These fears may persist until you remember the eternal nature of Soul and surrender your concerns to the Holy Spirit.

We Are Responsible

ECKANKAR teaches us to be responsible. On a physical level, this means we make every effort to support ourselves.

On a spiritual level, this means we earn our own state of consciousness.

This seems illogical if we view only one life at a time. In a single life we suffer or are blessed for no apparent reason. God seems arbitrary and random. The ECK principle of spiritual responsibility makes more sense as we accept the principles of karma and reincarnation. Reincarnation teaches that we are born again and again until we learn the spiritual lessons of life. The Law of Karma ensures that we link our behavior with its inevitable results. We reap in one life what we have sown in another.

If we impede the development of another human being, we will incur a karmic debt. By our actions, it's clear we haven't yet learned the Law of Love. The debt will have to be paid, and a lesson will have to be learned. The suffering which may follow is not the act of a vengeful God. We are just reaping what we have sown. It is the loving God which helps each Soul develop Its highest spiritual potential through experience.

Perhaps the most serious of karmic infractions is to misuse spiritual power for personal gain. History brims with examples of those who used psychic insight for personal advancement. False teachers have incurred a debt to their followers and at some point, that debt must be paid.

Experience Teaches Us

Experience teaches us. When a lesson is learned, particularly a spiritual lesson, we no longer need the experience. The karma is finished. We can move on to the next step. This is not absolution or forgiveness. It is spiritual growth.

Spiritual Maturity Comes When We Realize We Are the Creator of Our Own Life

We cannot purchase God Consciousness in a marketplace, nor can it be granted to us by another. Our mistakes or sins of the past cannot be absolved at the last minute simply by request. We earn spiritual wisdom by taking responsibility for our actions and by learning how the ECK, the Holy Spirit, works. Spiritual maturity comes when we realize we are the creator of our own life. We learn to be a Co-worker with God by understanding how to create what is highest and most beneficial for the whole.

5

Reincarnation

Each shall go through body upon body, reincarnation after reincarnation, until the day comes when he shall meet with me again in the body form in which I shall be known as the Mahanta. Only when he is ready and has reached perfection, when all dross has burned away and he has gained spiritual maturity, will he return to the heavenly fields and become a worker in the spiritual realms.

The Shariyat-Ki-Sugmad,
Book One

Another scientific principle is the conservation of matter and energy. This natural law states that matter can neither be created or destroyed; it can only be changed from one form to another.

French chemist Antoine-Laurent

Lavoisier discovered this principle in the late eighteenth century shortly before losing his head in the French Revolution. Since then, several scientists, including John Dalton and Albert Einstein, refined and expanded on the principle. They found that the total amount of matter and energy in the universe always remains the same. The parts are just reassembled into new combinations.

Every aspect of the universe is part of a phenomenal recycling effort. We, as Soul, are divine sparks of God. That which can never be created nor destroyed. This doesn't mean that the human population on earth remains the same. Not all Souls incarnate as humans at the same time.

We evolve in consciousness through many different forms of life, even in the plant and animal kingdoms, before we take human form. Our goals are to learn how to survive, how to love, how to achieve self-mastery, and how to find our way home to God.

Near-Death and Out-of-Body Experiences Have Helped People Live Life More Fully

Some people have had near-death experiences. They were able to view their injured body from above and had a glimpse of the higher worlds. Most have extremely happy and uplifting experiences.

Soul never dies. It does not grieve for Its physical body. Many tell of meeting old friends or relatives who have passed on or of encounters with great majestic beings who greet them but say the time for their death has not yet arrived. Those who return to their physical body often feel totally different about their lives. They are now free of the fear of death and are able to live life more fully.

And there are those who've had out-of-body experiences. These experiences are similar to the near-death experience but can occur under more ordinary circumstances. The person is able to shift his spiritual attention away from the physical realm and travel in the Soul body. After such experiences it is hard to be afraid of death because the continuity of life becomes so apparent.

Heaven Exists on Other Planes

When the physical body dies, Soul continues to exist on the other planes of God. Soul may stay on these other planes for a day, a thousand years, or more. This is dependent on Soul's mission, Its karmic obligation, and Its level of spiritual unfoldment. For many, this in-between time is heaven. The Astral Plane, for example, has sections which resemble all of the heavens described in the major religious traditions. You might find Saint Peter and the pearly gates, or the happy hunting grounds, or even visit the palace of Zeus, or Jupiter. On the Astral Plane you find what you expect, what you hope for, or what you fear.

Reincarnation Helps Explain Aspects of Our Personalities

Reincarnation provides an explanation for various elements of our personality. Why does a young child show great musical talent when his parents have none? The reason could be that these talents were developed in a previous life and a subtle memory persists.

If the awareness of Soul is maintained, living in the physical world can be joyous. However, members of ECKANKAR aspire to spiritual freedom. This means they may choose to reincarnate but are not compelled to do so. The Mahanta can guide Soul out of the worlds of illusion and help It rise above the Laws of Karma and Reincarnation.

Reincarnation Is a Widely Held Belief

Reincarnation is a widely held belief. Hundreds of millions of people, including most Hindus and Buddhists, believe that Soul inhabits many bodies over the course of time. ECKists believe that Soul enters the body at or around the time of birth. Without the entrance of Soul, the body could not survive.

Soul Is Always Moving Forward

Soul is always moving forward. It is never punished. It must simply obey the Law of Karma and will eventually learn from Its experience. It is rare for an individual who has attained the human state of consciousness to be reborn as an animal. This would slow the ability to learn, to unfold, and to graduate from the school of life.

We've Been Here Before

Most of us have lived before. Soul reincarnates on the physical plane again and again until It graduates from the school of physical life.

By choosing different bodies and different life experiences, Soul learns to view life from all sides. Living as male or female, as black or white, as rich or poor, for example, Soul tests and purifies Itself.

There Is a Reason for the Veil Separating Us from the Past

If we could remember all of our previous lives, the confusion would be overwhelming. To survive on this earth, we must be able to focus on our current identity and deal with day-to-day events. Divine Spirit protects us from confusion by pulling the veil over our memory when we are reborn.

We Often Return to Be with Family and Friends from Before

The patterns of karma often bring us into contact with those we have known before. This is a thread which runs between family and friends, neighbors and business associates. Your sister from ancient Egypt may be your father-in-law today. Your adversary from the Civil War may be your friend in this life.

Past-Life Memory Is Accessible

Through the Spiritual Exercises of ECK, you can remember past lives. You would remember those which have a bearing on this life, the ones which give you insight into your current spiritual problems. These records are stored on the Causal Plane. They can be viewed as easily as you would visit a library on the Physical Plane, as long as you are detached enough to handle the information.

The Physical Plane
Is a School of Life

We often return to the school of life on earth, or some other physical arena, to continue our spiritual education. Soul, in harmony with the Law of Karma, chooses Its next incarnation. We choose our parents and our circumstances because they suit our spiritual needs. From this perspective, Soul is not concerned with pain or pleasure, riches or power. It simply is looking for Its next spiritual experience and is compelled to balance Its karmic account.

Similarly, those of us who find ourselves on a spiritual quest have probably pursued these interests before. Many on the path of ECKANKAR have studied with previous ECK Masters. We find a glint of recognition in this life. Others have led lives committed to spiritual unfoldment and now find themselves ready to continue with the next step.

ECKists are not frantic to escape this world or avoid rebirth. As a Co-worker with God, Soul is never finished with Its work. But at a certain point It may no longer need to inhabit a physical body. Reincarnation will only continue for those who need or choose it. The Mahanta can guide Soul out of the worlds of illusion and help It rise above the Laws of Karma and Reincarnation.

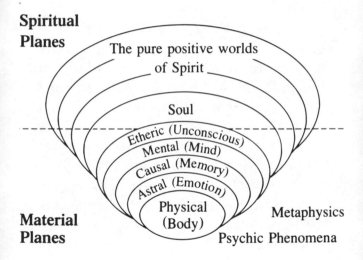

Spiritual Planes

The pure positive worlds of Spirit

Soul

Etheric (Unconscious)
Mental (Mind)
Causal (Memory)
Astral (Emotion)
Physical (Body)

Metaphysics

Psychic Phenomena

Material Planes

It is in these worlds that you take the journey from Self- to God-Realization.

6

The God Worlds of ECK

There is only a singular sense of purpose within the God Worlds, and this brings Soul into Its own reality. It separates illusions from truth and brings to Soul the recognition of Itself as a channel for the Mahanta. Soul establishes Itself in the true light of the SUGMAD by this recognition, and few, if any, will reach these heights unless they bring themselves to that point of getting rid of the ego and accepting the Mahanta as their spiritual guide in life.

The Shariyat Ki-Sugmad,
Book One

Years ago, a lone ECKist stood on a bridge over a river in Wisconsin. His story is a dramatic example of the ultimate experience of the Light and Sound, God-Realization. "From out of the night," he recounts, "as if from a distant lighthouse, came a searing bolt of blue-white light that pierced my heart. . . .

"A heavy roll of thunder shook the bridge, as if a locomotive were sweeping past a railroad crossing at high speed. I trembled at the power of the sound. . . .

"All became still. The sound of thunder ceased, but the Light and Sound of God poured endlessly into my heart as It swept down from the God planes, from the very center of creation. . . .

"Then it came, barely a breath of sound gliding over the water. . . . The soft ripple of sound washed in again. Without a doubt, it was ocean waves upon a peaceful shore. . . . The sound of waves grew still. A pause, then again the ocean swell, but this time more compelling. . . .

"The tide must be coming in, I thought. Faster, louder came the surging. Thunderous, booming, crashing. . . . With each tidefall I reeled. The full Ocean of Love and Mercy was crushing me, cleansing, scouring, blessing. . . .

"The Sound was All. It filled my every atom. The sweet and holy Current of God cradled me with Its fierce love. There was no part of me where it was not. This was the ECK, the ancient, ageless Voice of God, giving new life to Its creation."

That ECKist who stood on the bridge is Sri Harold Klemp. This experience, excerpted from his book *Child in the Wilderness,* occurred while he was in training to become the Mahanta, the Living ECK Master. His experience was dramatic and unique. Yet it shows what is possible for the seeker who loves God with all his or her heart.

Soul Travel Makes It Possible to Achieve God-Realization in This Lifetime

Learning to recognize, understand, and work with the Light and Sound of God is one of the most unique and exciting aspects of ECKANKAR. Becoming attuned to the sounds, visual characteristics, and vibrational rates of the God Worlds via Soul Travel makes it possible for the seeker to achieve Self-Realization and even God-Realization in this lifetime.

The God Worlds can best be described as planes of reality. Each plane corresponds to a certain state of consciousness and vibration. God, or the SUGMAD, is the source of all the planes. From out of the SUGMAD flows the ECK. It is the ECK, Divine Spirit, which supports and sustains all life in all planes.

Sri Harold experienced the Ocean of Love and Mercy in the pure spiritual worlds of God while physically on that bridge in Wisconsin. SUGMAD exists at the heart of the spiritual worlds, in the Ocean of Love and Mercy, beyond matter, energy, space, or time. It is in these worlds that you take the journey from Self- to God-Realization.

The Soul Plane

Self-Realization is achieved on the Soul Plane, just across the division between the higher (spiritual) and lower (psychic) worlds. The Soul Plane is the only plane in the higher worlds where Soul is still cloaked with a form or body. Each plane, whether psychic or spiritual, can be recognized by its own particular sound. The sound of the Soul Plane is the single note of the flute.

The ECK continues to flow outward from the heart of God, even to the far reaches of the lower worlds. These worlds are where we spend most of our time. They are the worlds of matter, energy, space, and time. The coarsest material level, operating at the lowest frequency of vibration, is the Physical Plane.

Life is short here, and the understanding of the spiritual laws is usually limited to a very few. As an ECKist, however, you learn that your experience is no longer limited to this plane. You also reach a point where, at the end of this lifetime, you may have a choice whether or not you wish to return.

Gain Spiritual Understanding from the Temples of Golden Wisdom

Often we gain wisdom and spiritual understanding by visiting Temples of Golden Wisdom. There are Temples on each plane, each with an ECK Master serving as guardian of the Shariyat-Ki-Sugmad, the holy scriptures of ECK. Most notable on the supraphysical and physical planes are the Katsupari Monastery in Tibet (Fubbi Quantz, guardian); the Gare-Hira Temple at Agam Des in the Himalayas (Yaubl Sacabi, guardian); the House of Moksha, the Temple on Retz, Venus (Rami Nuri, guardian); and the Temple of ECK, in Chanhassen, Minnesota (Harold Klemp, guardian). The sound of the Physical Plane is often heard as thunder.

The Astral Plane

As you dream, you may spend a great deal of time in a more refined state of consciousness called the Astral Plane. Your body is lighter and functions at a higher vibration. The Astral Plane is the source of human emotion, psychic phenomena, ghosts, and UFOs. The Astral Plane is also home for most humans upon the death of their physical body.

The Astral Plane is much larger and more beautiful than the Physical Plane and often mistaken for man's final resting place, or heaven. The spiritual beings who reside there seem angelic by earth's standards, and the rulers of the Astral Plane appear as gods to those unfamiliar with the planes above the Astral.

This is the highest plane reached by those practicing astral projection and most occult sciences. Askleposis, the Temple of Golden Wisdom on this plane, is located in Sahasra-Dal-Kanwal (Gopal Das, guardian). You can often recognize the Astral Plane by the sound of the roaring sea.

The Causal Plane

Memories of past lives are stored on the next higher plane of existence, the Causal Plane. If you are looking for the seeds of your current life, you could visit the Causal Plane and read the Akashic records. The Causal Plane contains more spiritual matter than does the physical, but it is still governed by the laws of duality. The Sakapori Temple of Golden Wisdom is located here in the city of Honu, and the guardian of the Shariyat-Ki-Sugmad there is Shamus-i-Tabriz. You can recognize the Causal Plane by the sound of tinkling bells.

As you travel into a higher state of consciousness, the magnificence of what you behold can be overwhelming. This in itself can be a trap, because the temptation to linger is strong. The impression is always that you have reached the highest state. This is why the Mahanta, the Inner Master is so important. He will always be near to give you a little nudge, to remind you to continue on your spiritual journey.

The Mental Plane

The source of the mind and its constructs—philosophy, ethics, and moral teachings—is the Mental Plane. It is a grand place populated by advanced spiritual beings. The word *Aum,* chanted by those in many religious groups, originates from the Mental Plane. Although this is a very spiritual plane, residents of this plane are still subject to reincarnation. This is because the Mental Plane is still part of the lower worlds.

To pass into the true spiritual planes, we must drop the mind. Soul uses the mind as a tool, but cannot be guided by it. The mind cannot understand the true nature of God. God can only be experienced, and descriptions of God are most often inaccurate because they depend on the power of the mind.

The Temple of Namayatan, the Temple of Golden Wisdom on this plane, is located in the city of Mer Kailash, and the guardian is the Koji Chanda. You can recognize the Mental Plane by the sound of running water.

The Etheric Plane

Marking the border between the lower and higher worlds of Divine Spirit is the Etheric Plane. This is the source of our subconscious, and primitive thoughts. The Dayaka Temple of Golden Wisdom is located here in the city of Arhirit, and the guardian of the Shariyat-Ki-Sugmad is Lai Tsi. You can recognize the Etheric Plane by the sound of buzzing bees.

As you unfold spiritually, you'll travel through the various God Worlds of ECK. This journey will be a unique experience because we are all individuals, each at a different point in our unfoldment.

7

Love

The very heart of the doctrine of ECK is love. This love is that divine essence which unites all reality and brings together all Souls. The higher Soul goes into the other worlds the greater this becomes. Love is the bond which holds the worlds together. It is the living ECK, the Spirit of the SUGMAD.

The Shariyat-Ki-Sugmad, *Book One*

A Minneapolis, Minnesota, newspaper once reported the story of a dog named Norman. Norman is very special. He's a shining example of divine love in action.

Norman, a curly haired cockapoo with weak knees, sports a different brightly colored scarf around his neck each day. He is a care giver at a south Minneapolis nursing home. An odd occupation for a dog? Not really, if you think about it.

He's good at what he does. Residents look forward to his arrival every day. He arrives in the morning with the activities director. He moves from lap to lap, day after day, giving selfless love and bringing joy to his patients.

Divine Love Needs No Words to Communicate

One patient in particular, who suffered a stroke, is especially appreciative of Norman's attention. She always welcomes him with a big smile and outstretched arms. They often set off for an adventurous ride in her wheelchair. The stroke took away her ability to speak, so she can't communicate with him verbally, but she scratches him on the head. Neither needs words to express the love they share.

Why does Norman take his job so seriously? Why does he do it so well and willingly? Because of the love he's been given.

When Norman was a pup many years

ago, he was abandoned on a doorstep. A loving Soul, his former master, rescued him. When it was discovered that he had leukemia, she invested over two thousand dollars of her own money to save him and nursed him back to health. It was then he began his career as pet therapist.

His master was associate director for a nursery and early childhood center. Many of the children were developmentally disabled. Norman's owner saw a bright future for him as a care giver. He charmed and inspired the children until his master died. That could have spelled the end of his career, but Divine Spirit and his master's sister saw more need for his gift of love. She started taking him to the nursing home where she worked, to continue his mission.

What Can We Learn from Norman about Divine Love?

The love given Norman by his master transcended the love most people give an animal. The love she gave was given with no thought of return. It was love given straight from the heart. Totally selfless.

This type of love keeps on giving, building on itself. Speaking of divine love, *The Shariyat* says, "One does not see and grasp it at first glance but it grows within him like the acorn of the oak in the earth. Gradually it opens the consciousness of the receiver and flows through to the world, changing all about it."

Further, it says, "The wise man is one who stores up the ECK within himself and at the same time distributes the spiritual love which is within himself. He is not one who gives his compassion to a few but to all, whether or not many understand this. He is able to live among the wretched, the thieves, the unhappy, robbers and fools, for he accepts life for whatever it is and gives love to all. He is the wise one who is able to give all that he has to his fellowman. He finds love for those who greedily accept what he gives, and they shall be blessed a thousand times for his love."

Life in the lower worlds is made possible by the interaction of two powerful forces: the ECK force and the Kal force. Positive and negative. Love and power. The ECK force descends from the pure positive worlds of God giving love and life to all that exists in the worlds below.

Love Is Simple

In *Cloak of Consciousness,* Sri Harold Klemp says, "It is no secret that the power of love is stronger than the power of the mind. The mind enjoys little games and psychic adventures, such as the use of crystal power. Someone who wants the God Consciousness no longer cares for these things. We care about the Light and Sound of God. For this one must have the Golden Heart, which means a heart filled with love.

"Someone told me about how well his young daughter took to having a new baby in the family. Whenever the baby wants the rattle or needs the bottle back in its mouth, the little girl simply helps the baby in whatever way she can.

"She doesn't question the reason for the baby's needs or wait to be told what to do. She does it simply because she loves the baby, with none of the petty jealousies that can make things complicated in a family or a group.... Love makes things very simple."

Know Greater Love through the Golden Heart

The key to love is the Golden Heart. If you have it, it is very easy to Soul Travel. Let's take a moment to look within and experience the radiant love of the Golden Heart.

Begin to visualize a growing, golden light surrounding you. It may be very subtle at first. It embraces you, flows with you.

Soon you are riding currents of light into the vastness of the cosmic sea. A place you've long forgotten. It's a place deep within your inner being, the dwelling place of Soul.

Now your consciousness settles on the surface of the sea. Now the sea of love and light begins to emanate from you, expanding. It's deeper than the mind can conceive. You've moved beyond the regions of space and time.

Ever so lightly, you sense a breeze. You hear the sound of a wind from deep within. It creates tiny ripples on the surface of the sea. Suddenly you realize you're experiencing the Light and Sound of God. You can stay here for a while if you choose, basking in this radiant, soothing ocean of Light and love.

When you're ready, slowly come back. It should be easy enough to speak of this kind of experience, but words often fail us. We can try to share our experience, but it's up to each of us to open up that awareness within ourselves.

Truth is not gained through observation, it's gained through experience. The

path of ECKANKAR offers each of us
the opportunity to open our consciousness and our hearts to greater awareness, to become the Golden Heart. We
can each feel the love that passes on from
one world to the next, into the higher
planes of reality. But the awakening has
to start within your heart.

8

The ECK-Vidya

A perfect record of every experience the individual has ever had in any incarnation within the countless ages of Its existence throughout any plane is stored here. These can be read by the Living ECK Master by use of the ECK-Vidya.

The Shariyat-Ki-Sugmad, *Book One*

In his book *Journey of Soul,* Sri Harold Klemp gives several important insights into the ECK-Vidya and the nature of prophecy through the following story:

"An individual had a question about the role of the ancient oracles in the spiritual life of man in the time of the Oracle of Delphi. To learn and open up, he decided to study the ECK-Vidya. First he went into a contemplative state and asked, 'What is this all about?' He then visualized himself in ancient Greece, sitting on the side of a mountain. After a while, an ECK Master came along and asked him what he wanted. He said he wanted an understanding about the role of oracles in the spiritual life.

"He came to understand that the oracles were used in those early times because the consciousness of man was so low. They were not able to go to the temple within directly, through the Spiritual Exercises of ECK, and meet the Inner Master to get the information on whatever they were looking for. So the ECK Masters at the time would work through oracles. What has come to us in history is a poor shadow of the original message that was given; it's merely a rehashing of the psychic and occult techniques which have lost their original meaning.

"As he sat there on the mountainside and got insight into his question, the ECK Master showed him some incidents from his past lives, revealing something that was of importance to him in this lifetime, something which had a direct bearing on his spiritual unfoldment. Little objects that looked like electromagnetic cards were pulled out of a file. You may either read them directly, or they may display pictures that give the complete scope of the individual and of those lives which were of importance. The ECK Master pulled these out for him and gave him a look. He considered this an added bonus, but it happened through his own efforts. He worked with his creativity to figure out how he could go about getting a deeper, more penetrating insight into his own life, and this is how he did it."

Man Always Wants to Know the Future

Men and women have long wanted to know what their future holds. They ask if they will be happy, find love, or become wealthy. They want to know about their health or their careers. Corporations spend millions of dollars trying to figure out the future. For the most part, they employ traditional forecasting methods. If they believed in the power of prophecy, they'd spend millions more to take advantage of it.

Many seekers of truth have the process of unfoldment in reverse order. They believe if one learns how to work with crystals, symbols, numerology, etc., they will unfold spiritually. In ECKANKAR, we believe one must first be linked with the Light and Sound of God. This process purifies Soul and enables us to become Co-workers with God. Once this occurs, we are able to work with the various tools and symbols offered by the ECK-Vidya. Without spiritual understanding, these items become playthings for psychic experimentation and do not lead to spiritual liberation.

All Life Is Cyclical

The ECK-Vidya teaches us that all of life can be divided into cycles. These cyclical patterns have their origins in the ECK, or Holy Spirit. Daily cycles are contained within monthly cycles, monthly within yearly, and so on. Because we understand earthly, physical cycles, we can predict when the moon will again be full. This would seem like a miracle to someone unfamiliar with the movement of the earth around the sun and the moon around the earth.

It is the same with spiritual cycles. All life is governed by spiritual cycles, and the ECK-Vidya adept comes to understand them. Prophecy becomes a natural talent. The cycles governing ideas, nations, and individuals become more clear.

ECK-Vidya Looks into Soul Records—Past, Present, and Future

Those trained in the ECK-Vidya are able to delve into the past and the future. These adepts can look into the Soul records to understand what has happened and why. They can also look into the future and see what is likely to happen. They can do this because they have come to understand the cycles of life.

This goes beyond astrology, which is the study of planetary influences only. Planetary influences are often overwhelmed by other spiritual forces at work. Knowledge gained from astrology originates from the Astral Plane, only one plane above the physical. The same can be said of other psychic procedures, like numerology or channeling.

This Is a Warring Planet, but That's OK

What does the future hold? Unfortunately for those utopians who believe we can have heaven on earth, our planet is a warring planet. Any period of peace will be followed by one of conflict. It is the nature of the lower worlds to have life and death, joy and suffering. The only way we can have heaven on earth is if our consciousness resides on the Soul Plane. Though we are in a physical body, our attention is on the love of God. Thus we are in this world, but not of it.

Never Use Knowledge to Manipulate Others

The ECK-Vidya has identified the various cycles which govern man's life here on earth. The responsibility of working with the ECK-Vidya is great, because the information gained can be so easily misused. Many people would be knocked out of balance if they knew what was going to happen to future generations. Others would try to take the information and use it for their personal financial advantage. A rule of Divine Spirit is that we must never use our knowledge to control or manipulate others.

Golden-tongued Wisdom

There are two elements of the ECK-Vidya which play a role in the life of the average person. These are called the

Golden-tongued Wisdom and the waking dream.

The Golden-tongued Wisdom is phenomenon which trains people to look for spiritual guidance in the most mundane of events. For instance, you could be shopping in a store when the clerk suddenly makes a casual remark to you. Though innocent enough in itself, the comment has some specific spiritual meaning to you.

It's as if the ECK is speaking to you through the unwitting channel of the store clerk. Or perhaps you turn on the radio and begin listening to the lyrics of a popular song. The message inspires you, and you see the solution to a current problem. With an open heart, you can hear the voice of Divine Spirit speaking to you through the Golden-tongued Wisdom.

The Waking Dream

A variation on the principle of the Golden-tongued Wisdom is the waking dream. The waking dream is another vehicle through which Divine Spirit communicates to you. But these experiences are more couched in symbols, similar to dream experiences.

Say a man is shown a picture of a butterfly, but in his mind it looks like a bee. A few hours later, he hears his wife mention the letter *B*. A week later, a friend asks if he is getting enough B vitamins. Now the connection between all three events becomes clear to him. He starts taking extra B vitamins, and a health problem he'd asked for help with improves.

Soul, the higher self, made sense of the symbolic events, and the message made its way to the conscious mind. This is an example of the waking dream.

To learn more about the theory and practice of the ECK-Vidya, you can read *The ECK-Vidya, Ancient Science of Prophecy* by Paul Twitchell. More specific information on the Golden-tongued Wisdom and the waking dream can be found in Sri Harold Klemp's books *The Eternal Dreamer* and *The Dream Master.*

9

Solving Problems

*N*o *problem is given man which is greater than himself. Each being is tested according to his capacity; none are tested beyond it. Each problem which man encounters has a spiritual solution, and each person has his troubles at the point where he is most negative and vulnerable.*

The Shariyat-Ki-Sugmad, *Book One*

In any subject you take in school, whether it's science, math, history, or art, the secret to success is problem solving. Generally, the solution is contained within the problem. The more experienced you become, the more problems you solve, the more you grow in mastery and confidence, especially with problem solving on a mental level.

The same is true in the school of life. Sometimes, however, the problems we face seem beyond our abilities. Here is our opportunity to grow spiritually. Knowing how to work with the ECK, Divine Spirit, helps us overcome the fear of facing something that seems beyond our ability. We live a much more joyful, fulfilling life. Knowing how to strike a balance between doing everything within our power to address a problem and handing it over to the ECK is the secret of problem solving from a spiritual perspective.

Whether the problems we face are financial or health related or spring from a lack of self-discipline, there are spiritual exercises to help us address them. The following are a couple of examples.

The Fine Art of Knowing When to Give Up

A short while ago, an ECKist found himself in a discouraging financial position. He looked at the stack of bills on his desk for mortgage, car payment, utilities, and credit cards. Then he looked again at his checkbook balance and projected his income for the month. He felt numb when he discovered he would be short several hundred dollars at least. Even if he paid some of the bills late, it wouldn't solve the problem. It seemed impossible.

To complicate matters, he soon found that his position with a large corporation was to be eliminated in several months because of downsizing. The company had just undergone a merger and was eliminating duplication. He'd been working diligently to seek out new opportunities for the survival of his family. They loved their little home in the country and the quaint community in which they lived. But it seemed nothing was working out.

Finally, he reached a point of surrender. "Mahanta," he said, "I've done all I can. I surrender this situation into your hands." Then he let go of his attachment to all of the problems he faced. He put his trust totally in the ECK and the Inner Master.

When he received his next paycheck, he discovered to his amazement that it included an extra two weeks' salary. A note accompanying the check explained that this was money that had been held out at the beginning of his employ by the old company he worked for before the merger. To help simplify bookkeeping, employees of that company were being reimbursed. The check contained enough money to cover the deficit he faced, with enough left over to get a jump on the following month.

In addition, he found a new permanent position with another company that turned out to be the best job he'd ever had. It meant leaving the large corporation, giving up his cherished home, and moving halfway across the country. But it also meant a more secure and spiritually fulfilling future for his whole family.

The HU Will Help You

There is little more frightening for a parent than the thought of a child getting lost or disappearing. A family of four was visiting Minnesota for the first time. They were from a small New England town and were unaccustomed to large, crowded shopping malls. One day during their visit, they decided to visit one of the huge malls the area had to offer. The two children, both boys, love to ride escalators. The boys spotted a long one, all silver and glass with black handrails. Steps rose out of the floor, moving gracefully and invitingly, one by one, up to the second floor. The boys begged to ride the escalator.

After they rode the escalator up, the boys took another back down. Then, amid the confusion of the crowds, the youngest boy got separated from his family. He disappeared. Dad, Mom, and the older brother scoured the mall for over a half hour with no success. It seemed an eternity. Finally, Mom did a spiritual exercise. She sang the HU. She took two steps then heard a tearful little voice behind her cry, "Mommy!" Her little boy stood with a security guard in exactly the same spot where she had sung the HU.

Use the Shariyat Technique for Well-Being and Happiness

If you have a problem you're having trouble solving using other techniques, this one has proved to be helpful to many ECKists. It's especially helpful if you are down-to-earth by nature. Called the Shariyat technique, this is given in Sri Harold Klemp's book *Unlocking the Puzzle Box.*

First, simply look at your problem. What is its nature? Is it a spiritual matter, or does it involve physical health, finances, or a broken heart?

Second, open Book One or Two of *The Shariyat-Ki-Sugmad* at random and read a paragraph.

The third step is to chant HU and contemplate upon what you have just read in *The Shariyat.* Don't contemplate on your problem or try to make some kind of a bridge between your paragraph and your problem. This is very important. Just contemplate upon the paragraph from *The Shariyat* while chanting HU.

After you have completed the contemplation, the fourth step is to open *The Shariyat,* again at random, and read another paragraph. At this point, you can try to see how the first and second paragraphs relate to your problem. The entire exercise shouldn't go much longer than fifteen or twenty minutes.

The following day, if you still don't have an answer, do this spiritual exercise again. If you do get an answer, then you can use the same technique on another problem bothering you.

10

Initiations

At the time of initiation the chela is imparted vital secrets, which facilitate his growth and speed up his karma. The highest, perfect directions for the Spiritual Exercises of ECK are given. These help him to unfold his inner hearing and inner sight, and with them he begins his ever growing inward and upward pilgrimage to the SUGMAD.

The Shariyat-Ki-Sugmad, *Book One*

A new ECKist from Australia had been wondering what her First Initiation would be like. When she was ready for it, a Higher Initiate in ECK came to her in the dream state and said, "Come, let us go see the Master." Together the new ECKist and the Higher Initiate journeyed to one of the worlds of the Astral Plane, chatting as they walked along. Soon the Master appeared in the Light body, and the First Initiation was given.

The individual went on to complete her second year of study, at which time she was ready for the Second Initiation. This one is given on the outer and the inner at the same time, and this is where the full linkup with the Holy Spirit occurs.

As she sat with the ECK Initiator in contemplation, she became aware that the Initiator was leading her down a beach. The setting was very familiar; she had been there in the dream state many times since childhood. Is this real or am I imagining it? she wondered.

All of a sudden her consciousness was fully on the inner plane. She and the Initiator were met by the ECK Master Rebazar Tarzs, who joined them in their walk along the beach.

Ahead of them on the sand was a blanket spread with fruit. The Inner Master, the Mahanta, was waiting for them. In his hands he held a goblet made of precious jewels. "This is the water of life," he said to her. "Take it, and drink."

This water of life is actually the ECK, which is the Light and Sound of God. Once a person drinks of it, he will never be the same. This is the sort of thing that occurs during the ECK initiation. You become aware that ECK is the path of love. When this connection between Soul and the Holy Spirit is made, it is simply to give the person the best opportunity to live his life in the most fruitful way possible.

Initiation Links Soul to the Audible Life Stream

The ECK is the essence of SUGMAD, or God. It flows from the Creator down into the lower worlds and then returns again to the Source. It supports and sustains all life. Over the centuries It has been given many names. The Holy Spirit, Holy Ghost, Logos, the Word, Divine

Spirit, the Bani, and the Vadan are a few of these names. Many religious traditions refer to the ECK in some way.

Divine Spirit is also called the Audible Life Stream, because It can be experienced audibly, as Sound. It is awareness of this Sound that distinguishes ECKANKAR from many other religions. When Soul is ready, the Mahanta links It with this Sound. This allows Soul to travel at Its own pace back to God.

As individuals progress spiritually, they become eligible for further initiations. Each initiation strengthens the bond of love between the individual and God.

How Many Initiations Are There?

The inability of the mind to comprehend those areas beyond the Soul Plane limits us in our understanding of the various heavens and their corresponding initiations. From the physical perspective, we can identify fourteen levels of initiation. Yet there is always a plus factor in ECKANKAR. There is no end to the spiritual universe. The God Worlds are not finite areas surrounded by borders.

Each of Us Enters ECKANKAR with a Different State of Consciousness

Each of us enters the path of ECKANKAR with a different state of consciousness. Our own level of unfoldment depends on our experience in this life and in previous incarnations. Some have studied the ECK teachings in past lives and therefore take to the path quite easily. For others it may be their first contact with the teachings of Light and Sound, and they may feel more comfortable proceeding slowly.

The Initiation Process

Beyond the First Initiation, which occurs in the dream state, initiations in ECK are given both physically and spiritually. The Living ECK Master authorizes each initiation. A letter is sent to the ECKist, which is an invitation to receive the initiation. The ECKist then makes an appointment with an ECK Initiator.

The initiation takes less than an hour to complete, and includes instruction and contemplation. In some initiations, a new spiritual word is given, to be sung during spiritual exercises.

Initiation Pace and Frequency Vary

The pace of spiritual progress varies from person to person. A number of years normally pass between ECK initiations to ensure that each person has built strong spiritual foundations at each level.

Some may experience their next initiation inwardly six months or more before they receive the outer invitation from the Master. For others, the significance of the initiation may not be fully understood for months after the initiation.

Each Initiation Corresponds to a Different Plane of Existence

Each initiation corresponds to a specific plane. The Second Initiation is related to the Astral Plane, the Third to the Causal Plane, the Fourth to the Mental Plane, and so on. The Fifth Initiation is especially significant, because it corresponds to the Soul Plane. This is the beginning of the pure spiritual worlds, above space and time. At the Fifth Plane, the usual laws of karma and reincarnation no longer hold sway.

Consciousness Has to Be Earned Moment to Moment

Of course, obtaining the Fifth Initiation in ECKANKAR does not guarantee spiritual balance or understanding. Consciousness always has to be earned moment to moment. Regardless of spiritual stature, a person can become confused, experience a spiritual setback, and have to start on the path again. The road becomes narrower as we move into the higher worlds. With greater spiritual freedom comes greater responsibility and accountability.

The Rules Change
from Plane to Plane

The initiations of ECK can have a dramatic effect on our spiritual lives. If, as a Second Initiate, we become accustomed to operating on the Astral Plane, we may expect the rules and systems learned there to work for us everywhere. Many who take the Third Initiation are puzzled to find that the Causal Plane operates in a different manner. They must learn the new rules. This process constitutes part of our spiritual growth.

The Real Initiation Occurs Inside

Only the Mahanta, the Living ECK Master can link up Soul with the ECK through initiation. The outer initiation is simple and easy. As with many experiences in ECKANKAR, the real event occurs inside each of us. The outer initiation is a physical acknowledgment of the inner spiritual event. It is the inner event which makes all the difference.

Initiations Are Private and Sacred

The clergy of ECKANKAR are from the ranks of the Higher Initiates, those in the Fifth Circle or above. And teachers of ECKANKAR classes must have received at least their Second Initiation. Yet these are not distinctions which one ECKist uses to compare himself to another, or to gain status in the community. The initiations of ECK are private and sacred.

Each Initiation Is an Invitation from the Living ECK Master to Take the Next Step on the Way Home to God

The Living ECK Master is the only one who can approve an initiation for an ECKist. The First Initiation usually comes within the first year of study. It is entirely an inner initiation. Sometimes the student of ECK will remember this, and sometimes not. It can occur in the dream state, or it can be experienced during a spiritual exercise. There is no outer ceremony to mark the First Initiation.

Each person, regardless of his outer initiation is capable of spiritual greatness. Each initiation is an invitation from the Living ECK Master to take the next step on the way home to God.

11

The ECK Masters

These ECK Masters are also on every plane and planet in the universes of God. Their work is to help forward the evolution of humanity, to find and train disciples. They see that these disciples come to the Living ECK Master so that he can take them under his charge to bring about the qualities of love and wisdom in this world.

The Shariyat-Ki-Sugmad, *Book Two*

Much has been written about guardian angels. In fact, there have been so many reports of angelic visitations that national research groups have been formed to record and investigate the phenomenon.

Sometimes these angels appear physically during a life-threatening episode, then disappear. Other times, accompanied by blue or white light, they appear in an inner vision or a dream. Sometimes they appear as invisible friends to children. One common thread in all these appearances is that, through the experience, people's lives were changed for the better.

In ECKANKAR, these angels are ECK Masters. You've read about several of them already. ECKANKAR literature is rich with the stories of people who were helped by the ECK Masters. They include inner healings by Lai Tsi, an ancient Chinese ECK Master. And accounts of animals or favorite pets being protected by Prajapati, another ECK Master. Their appearance makes an impression that lasts a lifetime. Often these occurrences took place before people discovered ECKANKAR for themselves.

Probably the most common occurrence is the appearance of the "man in blue" or the appearance of a blue light. This is the Living ECK Master.

The Living ECK Master Belongs to the Order of the Vairagi, Providing Guidance Home to God

When the Living ECK Master steps down from his position, he usually takes on a different mission in the heavenly hierarchy. Shamus-i-Tabriz, who served as the Living ECK Master over four hundred years ago, now teaches in a wisdom temple on one of the other planes.

The brotherhood of ECK Masters are members of the Order of the Vairagi. The Sanskrit word *vairag* means "detached." These Masters are detached from the passions of this world. Their only mission is to guide Soul home to God. They do not have a social agenda and usually stay away from political and other causes. Through the Spiritual Exercises of ECK, many ECKists work with some of these ECK Masters.

Sri Harold Klemp's Link with a Long Line of Living ECK Masters

The present Living ECK Master, Sri Harold Klemp, studied under Paul Twitchell, who studied under numerous teachers, including the Tibetan, Rebazar Tarzs. This unbroken chain reaches back through time. There have been countless ECK Masters in this lineage. Some have been historical figures, but most have worked silently or with small groups.

You Can Be Free from Fear

A common expression in ECKANKAR is that the Master is always with you. The Mahanta gives spiritual protection in a number of ways. Just like on earth, the inner heavens contain both good and bad elements. Some of us stumble onto certain areas of the Astral Plane and become frightened. Without knowing why, other people are plagued by fears throughout their life. And still others, particularly in the developing nations, have serious concerns about witchcraft and voodoo. The Mahanta provides a cloak of protection for his students so they can grow and learn spiritually without fear.

We Are Never Given
More Than We Can Handle

The Mahanta also works with each ECKist in the dream state. When we dream, we simply operate in a different state of consciousness. We have less resistance to Divine Spirit, and we can more easily receive the guidance of the Master. The ECKist finds many spiritual issues are resolved while dreaming, and ECKANKAR provides instruction which helps us remember and understand our dreams.

The Living ECK Master
Grants Total Spiritual Freedom
to His Students

The prime mission of the Mahanta, the Living ECK Master is to lead Soul home to God. The Master always grants total spiritual freedom to his students. They are never controlled or manipulated, and they have complete freedom of choice in every aspect of life. The ECK Masters have attained spiritual freedom for themselves and would like to share this joy with as many Souls as want it.

There Is Always a Living ECK Master

ECKANKAR always has a living Master. The Living ECK Master makes sure the spiritual essence of the teachings remains pure even though the outer form and shape of ECKANKAR might change.

Each Living ECK Master is responsible for training and appointing his successor. There are always a number of individuals who are quietly in training to become the next Living ECK Master. The spiritual training is rigorous, and many do not pass the required tests. Only one is chosen.

Few Religions Resemble the Spiritual Teaching Given by the Founders

Very few religions of today resemble the spiritual teaching given by their founders. Christianity has gone through many changes, and the Bible has seen many edits. As a result, the words spoken by Jesus sometimes bear little resemblance to what appears in the scriptures today. The purpose of a living Master is to prevent such misdirection of the original spiritual truths. The Master is the Living Word.

With the Living ECK Master as Guide, We Experience Only What Is Necessary for Spiritual Growth

The ECK Masters have made the same spiritual journey and have come to understand the road. They know the shortest route. We can save enormous wear and tear by following their lead back to God. Without a spiritual guide, the journey home can be long and arduous. With the Living ECK Master as our guide, we experience only what is necessary for our spiritual growth. The purpose of the Living ECK Master is to show us the way home to God.

The Mahanta Is the Inner Form of the Living ECK Master

The Mahanta, the Living ECK Master is the spiritual leader of ECKANKAR. The Mahanta is the inner, or spiritual, form of the Living ECK Master, which most ECKists work with on a daily basis. Few can physically converse with the Living ECK Master because of physical-world limitations. But the Mahanta is available to all at every moment.

The Living ECK Master Is Not Worshiped

In ECKANKAR, the Living ECK Master is not idolized. He is given respect and love, but he is not worshiped.

It is the Master's function, not his personality that is important. Thus when the Mastership is passed from one person to another, the spiritual life of the ECKist need not change.

The Living ECK Master Takes on Karma but Doesn't Relieve It

The Mahanta also takes over the karma of his followers. This does not mean he will relieve anyone of their karma, for this could mean they would be deprived of an experience they may need. But it means their karmic experience will be organized in such a way they can better understand the lessons being offered.

If we open our hearts, we will be able to see what our experiences are telling us about our attitudes and our own spiritual nature. The Mahanta also tells us we will never receive more than we can handle. Our karma is regulated in such a way that, if we listen to our spiritual guidance, we won't be overloaded, lose

our balance, and fall off the spiritual
path.

It's Natural to Question

The God Worlds of ECK are vast and
can be quite confusing to the uninitiated.
Am I on the Astral Plane? Am I on the
best path? Is this a true spiritual experience, or am I deluding myself? Where are
the signposts? How far is the goal? What
is the goal? It is natural under such circumstances to seek out a guide. We look
for someone who has traveled the road
before and can now show us the way.

The ECKist's Goal
Is Spiritual Mastery

The goal of every ECKist is to experience life to the fullest. That is spiritual
mastery. Some of us may eventually serve
on earth as "guardian angel" ECK
Masters, while others will pursue spe-
cialized interests in the spiritual worlds.

12

The Play of Soul

The play of Soul is like a drama in which Soul is both the actor and audience. On entering the theater the audience knows that it is about to see a play, but the actor creates maya, an illusion of reality which gives the audience extreme emotions of joy or terror, laughter or tears. It is in the joy and sorrow of all beings that Soul, as audience, is carried away by Itself as the actor.

The Shariyat-Ki-Sugmad, *Book One*

ECKANKAR Is a Living Religion

The great beauty of ECKANKAR is that it is a living religion. It's not bogged down with credos and dogmas. It evolves as our consciousness evolves. We do not worship the Living ECK Master. He is a guide to be respected, loved, and honored. He is not an icon to be worshiped. You may study many books and attend classes or lectures, but your real learning comes from inside yourself and from your experiences.

Prove It for Yourself

As reported in *The Shariyat-Ki-Sugmad,* the ECK Master Gopal Das once said, "Those who follow the ECK take nothing for granted, for they must prove it themselves. Only then will they know that God so loved them that He sent a Living ECK Master to bring Souls home to Him."

Understand Who You Really Are

As you begin to study the teachings of ECKANKAR, you may accelerate your spiritual growth. By practicing the Spiritual Exercises of ECKANKAR, you can

learn to Soul Travel. You begin to understand who you really are: that you're here
for a spiritual purpose. You can let go of
your fear of death. You worry less. You
invite more love into your life. You feel
energized, and grow and change. Unde-
sirable habits begin to fall away.

You begin to understand the nature
and importance of dreams. The dream
becomes a teaching tool. The Dream
Master is the teacher. He helps you look
unabashedly at your innermost fears and
desires, and helps you come to terms with
them. The ultimate purpose of dreams is
to bring you closer to the Light and Sound
of God.

Become Liberated
from Being the Victim

In time, past lives are revealed to you.
You discover the role of karma and reincarnation in spiritual unfoldment. You
become liberated from being the victim.
You learn you are responsible, but you

discover that the responsibility is not a weight. It is a key to spiritual freedom. You are the creator of your life; and by taking responsibility for your actions and learning from your experiences, you earn wisdom and spiritual maturity.

As your relationship with the Inner Master matures, you also become more aware of the God Worlds. You explore other planes, even other planets. You visit Temples of Golden Wisdom. You meet ECK Masters, and the universe opens up for you. The process of God-Realization begins. You let God enter more fully into your life.

Life Becomes Miraculous

When you let God into your life, divine love also enters. Experiences and coincidences you would have discounted as trivial before now, become miraculous. Life itself is rich, and you discover the joy of service and charity. God's love awakens your heart. You find this love in the eyes of the Living ECK Master and in the eyes of friends and family.

You'll be given the keys to the future and the past. Events and experiences will speak to you in a way you've never known before. You can begin to see cycles and connections between your life and timeless wisdom. The waking dream and Golden-tongued Wisdom open your inner eyes and ears to the Voice of God.

There Are Many Techniques, and Always the Inner Master, to Act as Your Light through the Darkness

Problem solving will one day cease to be as frustrating or traumatic. You come to understand that you are never given a problem beyond your abilities. You learn to hone your existing talents and develop new ones. Although growth seldom seems comfortable, the self-mastery you gain gives you a far deeper level of self-assurance and sense of comfort. You are never alone. There are many techniques, and always the Inner Master, to act as your light through the darkness.

To Become a
Member of ECKANKAR...

To become a member of ECKANKAR, you can call ECKANKAR at (612) 544-0066. Or you can write to ECKANKAR, P.O. Box 27300, Minneapolis, Minnesota 55427 U.S.A.

One of the benefits of membership is that you receive monthly discourses, or spiritual study lessons. During your first two years, you can choose to study dreams or spiritual exercises. You will unfold at your own pace. You can stay in your present religion. In fact, its teachings will probably become clearer than ever. You will probably notice an acceleration of change, but you'll always have the means at hand to understand why change is taking place.

With each year of ECK membership, you will receive new monthly lessons for your personal study. You can also join an ECK Satsang class studying any of the monthly lessons you have received. ECK classes offer a comfortable setting in which class members can share experiences, insights, and questions.

It is not until the end of a two-year period, when you're invited to receive your Second Initiation, that you decide whether to make a more lasting commitment to your spiritual awakening. After your Second Initiation, your life is transformed. You enter a new world of possibilities.

Love for and
Responsibility to All Life

Sri Harold says that "The teachings of ECK work on the simple principle that love is the divine current which makes all life possible. We as Soul ride on this current, first of all, away from God. Then, at the farthest point away, at the very end of Its rope, Soul finds the teachings of ECK and can return home.

"Before this, Soul has despaired of ever finding truth, of ever finding the best way home to God. Throughout Its many sojourns, in Its many lifetimes on earth and on the inner planes, Soul has been granted boons such as instant healings and 'undeserved' riches. All too often the individual has been misled to believe that life is a free ride or that life gives its bounties only to the fortunate. This misunderstanding has brought confusion.

"But when we come to ECK, we find that the games of illusion come to an end. We stop believing all the lies that say we can get something for nothing. Finally we reach the understanding that everything we do, everything that happens to us, is for our own spiritual good and of our own making. At the end of the road we realize that the spiritual path is about love for all, self-responsibility, and responsibility to all life."

Bibliography

Harold Klemp, *Child in the Wilderness* (Minneapolis: ECKANKAR, 1989)

——————, *Cloak of Consciousness,* Mahanta Transcripts, Book 5 (Minneapolis: ECKANKAR, 1991)

——————, *The Eternal Dreamer,* Mahanta Transcripts, Book 7 (Minneapolis: ECKANKAR, 1992)

——————, *The Golden Heart,* Mahanta Transcripts, Book 4 (Minneapolis: ECKANKAR, 1990)

——————, *Journey of Soul,* Mahanta Transcripts, Book 1 (Minneapolis: ECKANKAR, 1988)

——————, *Soul Travelers of the Far Country* (Minneapolis: ECKANKAR, 1987)

——————, *Unlocking the Puzzle Box,* Mahanta Transcripts, Book 6 (Minneapolis: ECKANKAR, 1992)

Paul Twitchell, *The Spiritual Notebook* (Minneapolis: ECKANKAR, 1971, 1990)

——————, *The Shariyat-Ki-Sugmad,* Book One (Minneapolis: ECKANKAR, 1970, 1987)

——————, *The Shariyat-Ki-Sugmad,* Book Two (Minneapolis: ECKANKAR, 1971, 1988)

119

Index

How to Take the Next Step on Your Spiritual Journey

Discover your own answers to questions about your past, present, and future through the ancient wisdom of ECKANKAR. Take the next bold, adventurous step on your spiritual journey, and learn how you can join ECKANKAR.

ECKANKAR can show you why special attention from God is neither random nor reserved for a few saints. It is for every individual. It is for anyone who opens the heart to Divine Spirit, the Light and Sound of God.

If you're searching for the secrets of life and the afterlife, Sri Harold Klemp, today's spiritual leader of ECKANKAR, and Paul Twitchell, its modern-day founder, have written a series of monthly discourses that give special Spiritual Exercises of ECK and lead you in a direct way to God.

Those who wish to study ECKANKAR, Religion of the Light and Sound of God, can receive these special monthly discourses which give clear, simple instructions for the spiritual exercises.

Through Membership in ECKANKAR You'll Discover:

1. The most direct route home to God through ECKANKAR's teachings on the Light and Sound of God. ECKANKAR brings the opportunity to gain wisdom, charity, and spiritual freedom in this lifetime.

2. The spiritual meaning of dreams, Soul Travel techniques, and ways to establish a personal relationship with Divine Spirit through study of monthly discourses. These discourses are available to the entire family. You may study them at home or in a class with others.

3. Secrets of self-mastery in a special letter to members and articles by the Living ECK Master in the *Mystic World,* a quarterly newsletter. In it are also letters and articles from members of ECKANKAR around the world.

4. Upcoming ECKANKAR seminars and other activities worldwide, new study materials available from ECKANKAR, and more, through special mailings. Join the excitement and fulfillment of attending major ECKANKAR seminars!

5. The joy of the ECK Satsang (discourse

study) experience through classes and book discussions. These classes enable you to share spiritual experiences and find answers about the ECK teachings with others in your community.

How to Find Out More

To request membership in ECKANKAR using your credit card (or for a free brochure on membership) call (612) 544-0066, weekdays, between 8:00 a.m. and 5:00 p.m., central time. Or write to: ECKANKAR, Att: Information, P.O. Box 27300, Minneapolis, MN 55427 U.S.A.

How to Request Books

On the following pages is a selection of books and audiocassettes mentioned in *ECKANKAR—Ancient Wisdom for Today.* **For fastest service, phone (612) 544-0066** weekdays between 8:00 a.m. and 5:00 p.m., central time, to request books using your credit card; or look under ECKANKAR in your phone book for an ECKANKAR Center near you. Or write: **ECKANKAR, Att: Information, P.O. Box 27300, Minneapolis, MN 55427 U.S.A.**

Earth to God, Come In Please . . .

A collection of stories and techniques from people who have become aware of a greater force operating in their lives. Their remarkable experiences brought profound lessons in love and spiritual freedom that changed their lives.

The Shariyat-Ki-Sugmad
Books One and Two

The Shariyat-Ki-Sugmad contains the wisdom and ecstatic knowledge of those planes of the spiritual worlds beyond the regions of time and space. To read and study this highly inspired book will give the reader an insight into the scriptures found in the Temples of Golden Wisdom.

Way of the Eternal

An illustrated version of *The Shariyat-Ki-Sugmad.* No matter your age, you'll begin to understand more clearly the teachings of ECK, yourself, God, and your place in the universe.

HAROLD KLEMP	HAROLD KLEMP	HAROLD KLEMP
Cloak of Consciousness	Unlocking the Puzzle Box	The Dream Master
MAHANTA TRANSCRIPTS/BOOK 5	MAHANTA TRANSCRIPTS/BOOK 6	MAHANTA TRANSCRIPTS/BOOK 8
You CAN replace your fears with God's love	Your Spiritual Toolkit for the 1990s	Dream your way home to God

The Mahanta Transcripts Series

By Sri Harold Klemp

This collection of talks from around the world by the Living ECK Master contains hundreds of stories and spiritual exercises to help you learn:

- to experience yourself as Soul
- to discover how God speaks to you
- how Divine Spirit works with you
- how to live a more loving and creative life
- how to replace your fears with God's love
- how to open yourself to new spiritual horizons
- how to learn from your dreams
- that you are the creator of your own worlds

Titles of the Mahanta Transcripts Series include:

Journey of Soul, Book 1
How to Find God, Book 2
The Secret Teachings, Book 3
The Golden Heart, Book 4
Cloak of Consciousness, Book 5
Unlocking the Puzzle Box, Book 6
The Eternal Dreamer, Book 7
The Dream Master, Book 8
We Come as Eagles, Book 9

Sri Harold Klemp's
Three-Part Autobiography

These three books present Sri Harold's explorations of the spiritual life, how he worked toward Mastership in ECK, and how he attained God Consciousness. Titles are:

The Wind of Change
Soul Travelers of the Far Country
Child in the Wilderness

The Spiritual
Exercises of ECK
By Sri Harold Klemp

This incredible little book is a staircase with 131 steps. It's a very special staircase, because you don't have to climb all 131 steps to get to the top. And what awaits you at the top? The doorway to spiritual freedom, self-mastery, wisdom, and love.

ECKANKAR—The Key to Secret Worlds
By Paul Twitchell

One of the first texts on ECKANKAR and the Ancient Science of Soul Travel. It offers you simple exercises to understand the hidden forces at work in your daily life.

The Spiritual Notebook
By Paul Twitchell

Learn what saints and mystics knew about God and the Divine Force—the inspiration for all myths and religions. Whatever your religious belief, this book can inspire the beginning of your own inner journey.

The Tiger's Fang
By Paul Twitchell

Paul Twitchell's teacher, Rebazar Tarzs, takes him on a journey through vast worlds of Light and Sound, to sit at the feet of the spiritual Masters. Their conversations bring out the secret of how to draw closer to God—and awaken Soul to Its spiritual destiny.

HU: A Love Song to God

This two-tape audiocassette set is designed to help listeners of any religious or philosophical background benefit from the gifts of the HU. It includes an explanation of the HU, stories about how the HU works in daily life, and exercises to uplift you spiritually.

Dreams, A Source of Inner Truth

Dreams are windows into worlds beyond the ordinary. This two-tape audiocassette set can help you open these windows through insights and spiritual exercises given by Sri Harold Klemp, spiritual leader of ECKANKAR.

The ECK-Vidya, Ancient Science of Prophecy
By Paul Twitchell

The ECK-Vidya teaches us that life flows in cycles. These cyclical patterns have their origins in the ECK, the Holy Spirit. This book introduces ways to recognize the flow of Divine Spirit in the cycles of your life.

There May Be an ECKANKAR Study Group near You

ECKANKAR offers a variety of local and international activities for the spiritual seeker. With hundreds of study groups worldwide, ECKANKAR is near you! Many areas have ECKANKAR Centers where you can browse through the books in a quiet, unpressured environment, talk with others who share an interest in this ancient teaching, and attend beginning discussion classes on how to gain the attributes of Soul: wisdom, power, love, and freedom.

Around the world, ECKANKAR study groups offer special one-day or weekend seminars on the basic teachings of ECKANKAR. Check your phone book under **ECKANKAR**, or call **(612) 544-0066** for membership information and the location of the ECKANKAR Center or study group nearest you. Or write **ECKANKAR, Att: Information, P.O. Box 27300, Minneapolis, MN 55427 U.S.A.**

☐ Please send me information on the nearest ECKANKAR discussion or study group in my area.

☐ Please send me more information about membership in ECKANKAR, which includes a twelve-month spiritual study.

Please type or print clearly   141

_____

Name

_____

Street   *Apt. #*

_____

City   *State / Province*

_____

ZIP / Postal Code   *Country*